1001 WAYS TO
PATIENCE

D1121245

ARCTURUS

With special thanks to Anne Moreland

ARCTURUS

This edition published in 2012 by Arcturus Publishing Limited
26/27 Bickels Yard, 151–153 Bermondsey Street,
London SE1 3HA

ISBN: 978-1-84858-550-8
AD00AD002248EN

Printed in China

Contents

Introduction

Patience is one of the most important qualities we can develop in life. Without patience, we may be in danger of missing all sorts of opportunities that come our way, whether in terms of career advancement, building happy families, making – and keeping – friendships, or fully enjoying our leisure time. Instead of slowly but surely working towards goals, whatever they may be, impatient people give up too easily, angry with themselves

and others because the results they seek are not seen immediately.

   In order to achieve our aims in life, or simply to enjoy it in all its richness and variety, we all need a great deal of patience: for example, in learning a new skill; caring for a child; maintaining a friendship; embarking on a creative hobby or new sport. As is plain from watching children grow up, few of us are born patient: it is something we have to learn. This little book will cause you to reflect on this essential quality, and hopefully help you on your path to becoming a more patient, persevering, and determined person.

What is Patience?

We all think we know what patience is – self-control, the ability to keep calm, to wait, to endure, and to persevere. But it's also much more than this; it involves toleration, humility, love, respect, and confidence, not only towards others, but towards yourself – as you will find out here.

Patience: the ability to tell yourself, don't get angry, don't try to hurry. Take your time, do whatever you have to do properly and with care, and you will get there in the end.

There is a time for patience, and a time for action.

Why hurry along the path of life when you can slow down and take in the view?

Patience is the ballast of the soul that will keep it from rolling and tumbling in the greatest storms.
Bishop Hopkins

If you try to rush, you may make mistakes, which will take more time to rectify than you save.

Patience doesn't come naturally. It's something we learn, along with kindness, care, and thinking of others.

When you feel impatient, take a deep breath and count to ten. When you get there, if you still feel impatient, count back down to one!

If you're always in a hurry, your life will speed by very fast. Slow down, and the days will slow down with you.

Patience is not only a virtue, but an acquired trait.

Christian Calhoun

Losing your patience is not the end of the world. But only do it very occasionally, or it will mean nothing.

Waiting; hoping; believing; having faith. That's patience.

Remember, you only have to succeed the last time.

Brian Tracy

Trying to force people or events to go your way can be destructive. You may find that if you do, you will end up losing the opportunity to get what you want.

Listening to others, trying to understand them, thinking of them rather than yourself before you act, takes a rare kind of patience and self-knowledge, which few of us possess.

Fools rush in where angels fear to tread.

Alexander Pope

Little children have no patience; nor do childish adults.

When a patient man is goaded into anger, his anger may be deeper than that of someone who loses his temper every day.

17

Those who care deeply, whether for a person or a cause, will show patience, determination, perseverance, and endurance.

You can't see plants growing – unless you speed up a film – but you know that they do. Each day, tiny changes take place. It's the same with your life.

Patience can't be acquired overnight. It's just like building up a muscle – you have to work on it.

Eknath Easwaran

Pave your path to spiritual enlightenment with patience and love.

Being able to talk to a kind and patient friend, who will give sound advice, is one of the greatest blessings in life.

Patience is sitting back instead of hitting back.

Patience makes lighter
What sorrow may not heal.
Horace

The act of teaching involves forbearance – both on the part of the pupil and the teacher.

An impatient person is like a child – only able to see their own needs, rather than understand the limitations of others to fulfil them.

Let him that hath no power of patience retire within himself, though even there he will have to put up with himself.

Balthasar Gracián

Some people are naturally calmer than others. That just means that the more impetuous among us have to work harder to achieve patience.

Show patience, even when you don't feel it.

It can take patience to achieve our goals. And, indeed, patience to find out what our goals in life may be.

Patience is the guardian of faith, the preserver of peace, the cherisher of love, the teacher of humility. *Bishop Horne*

There are many reasons as to why people fail, but only a few as to why they succeed: hard work, determination, and patience.

Patience is often just as important as ability. Talented people often fail to achieve their potential because they lack the confidence and patience to deal with life's setbacks.

Procrastination is a way of wasting time; having patience is a way of using it wisely.

Have patience with yourself, as well as with others. Start by forgiving yourself your faults; only then can you begin to change them.

If you want things done yesterday, you'll probably find they won't get done until tomorrow.

Have patience and endure; this unhappiness will one day be beneficial. *Ovid*

Being right is not always as important as being patient. There is a time and place to speak your mind frankly, and it's seldom every day.

Many of the difficulties in our lives are not brought about by circumstance, but by our own impatience.

Be patient with your family and friends. Love them in spite of their faults… as they do you.

Though patience be a tired mare, yet she will plod.
William Shakespeare

Kind, quiet, patient people don't always get attention. That's because they don't seek it. Instead, they gain satisfaction from helping others.

Patience consists of always being a little more forbearing than you think you can be.

Don't always try to control events. Sometimes, you can afford to relax, and allow life to happen to you.

By time and toil we sever
What strength and rage could never.
Jean de la Fontaine

Life is a gift. Don't tear off the wrapper impatiently. Open it carefully, savouring each moment of curiosity and wonder.

Peace cannot be gained without patience.

Most of us are irritated every day by small things in our lives that are not quite right. Keep these imperfections in perspective, recognizing that they are not that important.

Patience pours oil on troubled waters.

Still achieving, still pursuing,
Learn to labour and to wait.
Henry Wadsworth Longfellow

The five steps to patience:
Being quiet and attentive
Listening
Thinking
Understanding
Controlling one's emotions

You can chase a butterfly all round a field, but you will never catch it. But if you sit quietly, it may alight near you, so you can study it.

Slow and steady wins the race.

Patience is not just something you feel; it's something you do.

Patience is not simply caution; it carries with it an element of divine grace.

Accept advice with patience, even if you have not the slightest intention of following it!

Perhaps there is only one cardinal sin: impatience. Because of impatience we were driven out of Paradise, because of impatience we cannot return. *W.H. Auden*

Watch a cat stalk a bird, and learn that the hunter always has more patience than its prey.

Even animals show patience; so why can't we?

With time and patience, we can begin to unravel the plot of our lives, and come to understand our most troubling emotions.

Being attentive to each
moment in the day;
not judging how you feel,
but letting your thoughts
pass by; resisting the chatter
inside your head. This is
being mindful, and
it requires great patience.

**We usually learn to wait when we no
longer have anything to wait for.**

Marie von Ebner Eschenbach

Practice makes perfect.

**Learning to relax can be hard work –
if being patient is hard work for you.**

If I keep a green bough in my heart, the singing bird will come.

Chinese proverb

When the going gets tough, the tough get going.

Patience is not just about the self. It's about other people, too, and how much attention one pays to their needs.

It's not that I'm so smart. It's just that I stay with problems longer.
Albert Einstein

**Patience is waiting.
Not waiting passively –
that's idleness – but the
perseverance to keep moving
forward when the road is hard.**

**All things come to he who waits …
provided he knows what he's waiting for.**
Woodrow Wilson

Knock at the door and it will open. Kick it, and most likely it will remain closed.

There is no forgiveness without patience and love.

Patience is life's shock absorber.

You can't judge a book by looking at the cover. Instead, open it, and find out what is inside.

Everyone ought to bear patiently the results of his own conduct.

Plato

Patience isn't just about standing still; it's about standing back.

Don't expect too much from others. Instead, learn to watch them patiently, so that you will find out what they can and can't do. That way, you won't be disappointed.

Patience demands courage:
to believe in yourself, and
to believe in others.

The best things in life are well worth waiting for.

Hurrying and scurrying, buzz and activity, may give the impression that much work is going on; but often, it masks the fact that very little is being achieved.

Invest in time, rather than spending it.

It is not necessary for all men to be great in action. The greatest and sublimest power is often simple patience.

Horace Bushnell

Pulling at an olive won't make it ripen faster.

Italian proverb

Patience is not a destination; it is a journey.

Even the simplest, most everyday object made with love, care, and patience, is something to treasure.

Endurance is the crowning quality And patience all the passion of great hearts. *James Russell Lowell*

Love lends patience; and patience love.

Find within yourself the patience of nature: the stillness of the mountain; the strength of the wind; the steadiness of the tide; the beauty of the night sky; the peace of dawn.

When you show anger and impatience, it's hard for others to tell whether your cause is just.

Patience is a secret garden carried in the heart.

The ability to be patient shows others that we value and care for them; being impatient tells them that we have no real interest in their thoughts and feelings.

Being persuasive means being patient.

53

Teach me the patience of unanswered prayer.

George Croly

Sharp words are only effective if seldom used.

It's no good telling a toddler to hurry down the street. For him or her, everything is new. Instead, be patient, and try to see how the world looks through a child's eyes.

You will never have a greater or lesser dominion than that over yourself.
Leonardo da Vinci

When you have too much to do, ask yourself, what will happen if I don't achieve my goal today? Will it be the end of the world? If not, give yourself permission to slow down a little.

In trying to live life to the full, don't make the mistake of cramming too much in. That way, the days will pass far too quickly.

Patience! Why, it is the soul of peace; of all the virtues it is nearest kin to heaven; it makes men look like gods.

Thomas Dekker

Mother nature, time, and patience, are the three best doctors. *Bulgarian proverb*

Patience is that little voice in your head saying, Be careful. Don't act right now. Wait until later, when you can think it over.

Have confidence in yourself. Take your time. March to the beat of your own drum.

Patience means changing yourself before you try to change the world.

**Patience with others is Love;
Patience with self is Hope;
Patience with God is faith.**

Adel Bestavros

In the rush to achieve, we often forget that patience not only shows true faith in ourselves, but is more likely, in the long run, to get results.

There is no progress without patience.

Patience is distinct from resignation. Patience is the belief that, in time, you will achieve your aims; resignation, that most likely you will not.

Patience is the universal equalizer in life between now and eternity.

Jesse Gause

Patience is a beautiful prayer.

The slower the pace, the longer the chase.

If love is a sickness, patience is the remedy. *African proverb*

Beware of undertaking too much at the start. Be content with quite a little. Allow for accidents. Allow for human nature, especially your own.
Arnold Bennett

Move ahead; but make sure to look back sometimes, and see how far you have come.

The Path to Patience

None of us start out in life with patience – it is something we have to learn, often through experience, and making mistakes. In this section, we look at how we can begin to make patience a habit, and through doing so, how we can perhaps start to relax and enjoy life a little more.

Patience is a form of respect: for others, and for oneself.

If you want those around you to be happy, start by being patient towards them.

Look before you leap.

Muddy water is best cleared by leaving it alone.
Alan Watts

**Wisdom in the man
Patience in the wife
Brings peace to the house
And a happy life.**

For true friendship to blossom, at least one person must be patient.

In prosperity, caution; in adversity, patience.
Dutch proverb

Patience breeds respect, courage, kindness, creativity, and the free play of the imagination. Impatience breeds anger, fear, self-absorption, and a sense of impending failure.

Patience is enduring love; experience is perfecting love; and hope is exulting love.

Alexander Dickson

Slowly, slowly, catchee monkey.

To cultivate the life of the mind, one must proceed slowly, with immense patience.

Patience must be coupled with firm boundaries. Otherwise, it all too easily leads to being taken for granted.

Nature thrives on patience; man on impatience.

Paul Boese

Rushing to achieve a goal may result in having to go back to the beginning, and starting all over again.

Amid the hustle and bustle of life, take time to savour the beautiful moments of a day: the rising of the sun; the singing of the birds; the green of the grass and the trees; the changing colours of the clouds and the sky.

With time and patience, the mulberry leaf becomes a silk gown.

Chinese proverb

Patience nourishes hope, faith, and belief.

It takes patience and observation to notice the many possibilities and opportunities that lie before you.

If we could have a little patience, we should escape much mortification; time takes away as much as it gives.

Marquise de Sévigné

When you become angry, you are expressing your impatience with yourself, just as much as with others.

Where there's a will, there's a way.

If you cannot be patient, you will never achieve what you wish for in life.

Inaction may be the biggest form of action.

Jerry Brown

With patience, you can assemble a group of people around you who will support and help you throughout your life.

When all your desires are distilled
You will cast just two votes
To love more, and be happy.

Hafiz of Persia

Patience is trust.

Jumping to conclusions is a destructive type of impatience; it can damage your relationships with other people, and your ability to make sensible decisions in life.

A lawyer needs three bags: one full of papers, one full of money, and the other full of patience. *French saying*

In modern life, there is always a great deal of pressure to do too much. Make sure you create moments in your day when you do nothing at all, so that you can reflect on what is happening around you.

Teach patience to your children; practise it also, or they will never learn it.

It is in the everyday and the commonplace that we learn patience, acceptance, and contentment. *Richard J. Foster*

Everyone wants to succeed; but few people are willing to invest the time, effort, and patience that are required to do so.

Be ever eager to learn – especially from your mistakes.

Don't criticize yourself too harshly – there are always plenty of other people who will do that. Instead, be as patient with yourself as you would like to be to others.

One minute of patience, ten years of peace.

Greek proverb

Age alone does not bring patience; for patience must be cultivated throughout life, with love and care, like a garden.

The curious paradox is that when I accept myself just as I am, then I can change.

Carl Rogers

If you replace worry with patience, you can begin to start solving your problems, one by one, step by step.

Sometimes, people would rather remain unhappy and frustrated than bend to the difficult task of facing reality, which requires courage and patience.

Education is the best provision for the journey to old age. *Aristotle*

**There is no path to patience.
Patience is the path itself.**

Patience begins with tears
and ends with a smile.
Spanish proverb

Those who try to achieve everything, achieve little; those who acknowledge their limits are more likely to succeed.

There is no short cut to patience; you must keep following the main road ahead.

In a spiritually sensitive culture, then, it might well be that age is something to be admired or envied.

Rowan D. Williams

Babies grow frustrated when they cannot have what they want; that is because they are helpless and dependent. Adults must learn to curb their frustration, and take control of their destiny.

Patience is not a right, or a gift that is granted; it must be earned, by application and perseverance.

Self-control, self-discipline, and self-respect are the three stepping stones to patience.

If you add a little to a little, and then do it again, soon that little shall be much.

Hesiod

Patience is its own reward; impatience its own punishment.

Building a house on solid foundations takes time and patience; but without such foundations, the house cannot stand.

The sweetness of patience helps counteract the bitterness of loss.

The herb patience does not grow in every man's garden.

Danish proverb

A patient mother; a kind father; the experience of being loved and cared for as a special person, day to day, hour to hour. What more does a child need to flourish?

Ask not what tomorrow may bring, but count as blessing every day that fate allows you. *Horace*

Patience is not the enemy of ambition but its true, loyal, and honest friend.

For peace of mind, resign as general manager of the Universe.

Larry Eisenberg

The devil is in the details, as the saying goes. So be patient, and search for the hidden catch.

Don't postpone your happiness;
that's a way of postponing your life.

Be patient, my
friends; time rolls
rapidly away; our
longing has its end.
The hour will strike,
who knows how
soon? *Friedrich Krummacher*

There is a place for righteous anger, when you suffer injustice. But express yourself with dignity, or your cause will be lost.

Science is not a discipline where great discoveries are made every day; it moves forward very slowly, inch by inch, thereby adding to our store of knowledge.

Patience is a tree with bitter roots that bears sweet fruits.
Chinese proverb

The seven heavenly virtues:
Valour: the pursuit of knowledge
Generosity: the pursuit of charity
Liberality: the pursuit of will
Diligence: the pursuit of ethics
Kindness: the pursuit of love
Humility: the pursuit of modesty
Patience: the pursuit of peace

Before you can control others, you must first be able to control yourself. Restraint is the key.

Every seed knows its time.

Deferred gratification: the ability to wait for what we want, instead of grabbing it right now.

A cool breeze against your cheek; warm sun on your shoulders; still water in a pond. These are nature's reminders to us to be quiet, patient, and grateful for being alive.

Patience is the mother of a beautiful child.
African proverb

Allowing yourself to rest from time to time does not mean letting go of what you desire in life – in fact, if you take regular breaks to recharge your batteries, you may find you work more effectively.

Patience is love in its practical form.

An impatient person may not be in the wrong, but he or she will always give the impression of being so.

Take pride in everything you do,
however mundane it may seem.
Working with love and care is a
much more enriching experience
than being slapdash in your tasks.

Better to light a candle than curse the darkness.

Chinese proverb

There are many paths to the top of the mountain, but the view is always the same.

Everything comes gradually and at its appointed hour.
Ovid

Patience makes a friend of time.

Take the opportunity to notice the miracles of life that are all around you.

The world is full of magical things patiently waiting for our wits to grow sharper.

Bertrand Russell

Beware of following your instincts; never rush into a decision.

Patience cannot make time stand still, but it can help to slow it down.

Like farmers, we need to learn that we cannot sow and reap on the same day.

Patience is a necessary ingredient of genius.

Benjamin Disraeli

Impatient, impulsive, impetuous; or patient, persevering, and polite?

It takes time to deal with trouble.

Don't think about how slowly things change; concentrate instead on the job of making small changes permanent.

Patience and self-belief will help you to go your own way, regardless of the advice and opinions of other people.

Without patience, there is no real affection.

Not all the thoughts that run through your head are useful; but, with patience, you can begin to pay attention to those that are worth heeding.

Each moment of your life is potentially a creative one: to make, or to learn something new.

If you want to make the most of life, develop a habit of patience. It will help you to see what matters, and what is insignificant.

Most men pursue pleasure with such breathless haste that they scurry past it.

Søren Kierkegaard

Patience is the level of endurance one can attain before despair sets in.

However difficult life is, we always cope better by being determined to make the best of the situation.

Contentment and patience are partners in life.

Be patient enough to answer simple questions; and patient enough to ask them.

An invulnerable armour is patience.
Buddha

In most instances, patience achieves more than force; and its achievement is more lasting.

Patience is the self-control to refuse, when that is the right thing to do.

The years teach what the days never know.

Ralph Waldo Emerson

Instead of pointing the finger, extend the hand.

Happiness and contentment are the fruits of patience and perseverance.

All animals and humans are inclined to favour short-term rewards; it is the work of patience to recognize that long-term rewards yield greater benefits.

Impatience is a denial of reality; patience an acceptance of it.

Trying to force the pace can only hinder it.

No man can learn patience except by going out into the hurly-burly world, and taking life just as it blows. Patience is but lying to, and riding out, the gale.

Henry Ward Beecher

Like charity, patience begins at home.

Peace occurs naturally when activity stops.

It's easy to find reasons why other folks should be patient.
George Eliot

Act quickly; think slowly.

Greek proverb

As you go through the forest, be sure to notice the firewood; you may be able to come back later and collect it.

If you do not grow up with patient parents and teachers, you have to learn patience by yourself, as an adult.

Your judgements about other people may tell the world more about you than them.

The bigger the dam of patience, the worse the flood when it breaks.

Austin O'Malley

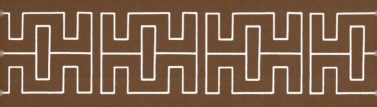

If you are not a naturally patient person, don't criticize yourself harshly for it. Instead, learn to recognize who you are; take your weakness into account in your dealings with people, and try to change.

Patience is knowing that behind the clouds, the sun may still be shining.

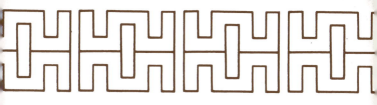

Failure, difficulty, and loss may provide unexpected opportunities; but it takes patience to see them.

Patience is a virile virtue; it does not mean lying down under affliction, but standing up under it, and marching on.

Walter Lowrie

Impatience is a child's reaction to frustration; patience an adult's.

Patience is a candle in the window, shining in the night, guiding the traveller back home.

Passivity and patience do not always go together; sometimes, patience is a form of resistance.

From the mystical to the mundane, patience has its special role to play.

The ability to wait, but to wait with hope, love, and confidence: that is true patience.

Patience is being friends with Time.

Vanna Bonta

Being patient is a question of sailing on calmly through the stormy seas of your emotions.

A journey of a thousand miles begins with one small step.

Chinese proverb

Patience and fortitude withstand all challenges.

Never cut what you can untie.

Joseph Joubert

Patience is not passive; on the contrary, it is active, concentrated strength.

Edward Bulwer-Lytton

Patience is a way of life, not just a technique to be practised.

The Guides

Patience is perhaps one of the most overlooked but important qualities of character. For centuries, scholars, poets, philosophers, and artists have written down their thoughts on patience, and offered us their advice not only on how to acquire it, but also on how to maintain it. Here are some of their reflections, both from the distant past and from anonymous sources.

Adopt the pace of nature: her secret is patience.
Ralph Waldo Emerson

There are two cardinal sins from which all others spring: Impatience and Laziness.

Franz Kafka

The shorter our time, the greater our capacity for waiting. *Elizabeth Taylor*

We could never learn to be brave and patient if there were only joy in the world.

Helen Keller

Be patient towards all that is unsolved in your heart, and try to love the questions themselves. *Rainer Maria Rilke*

The important thing is this:
to be ready at any moment to
sacrifice what you are for what
you could become.

Charles Dickens

Act with kindness, but
do not expect gratitude.

Confucius

Be courteous to all but intimate with few; and let those few be well tried before you give them your confidence.

George Washington

Patience is something you admire in the driver behind you and scorn in the one ahead.

Mac McCleary

Seek patience and passion in equal amounts. Patience alone will not build the temple. Passion alone will destroy its walls.

Maya Angelou

He preacheth patience that never knew pain.

H. G. Bohn

If you begin to understand what you are without trying to change it, then what you are undergoes a transformation.

Jiddu Krishnamurti

Patience is the key to paradise.

Turkish proverb

It takes patience to appreciate domestic bliss; volatile spirits prefer unhappiness.

George Santayana

Patience is also a form of action.

Auguste Rodin

Everything that slows us down and forces patience, everything that sets us back into the slow circles of nature, is a help. Gardening is an instrument of grace.

May Sarton

Patience is a most necessary qualification for business; many a man would rather you heard his story than granted his request.

Lord Chesterfield

Patience and diligence, like faith, remove mountains.

William Penn

Trust has to be earned, and should come only after the passage of time.
Arthur Ashe

Patience: a minor form of despair disguised as a virtue.

Ambrose Bierce

Making your mark on the world is hard. If it were easy, everybody would do it. But it's not. It takes patience, it takes commitment, and it comes with plenty of failure along the way. The real test is not whether you avoid this failure, because you won't. it's whether you let it harden or shame you into inaction, or whether you learn from it; whether you choose to persevere. *Barack Obama*

Genius is nothing but a great aptitude for patience.

Georges-Louis Leclerc, Comte de Buffon

A garden is a grand teacher. It teaches patience and careful watchfulness; it teaches industry and thrift; above all it teaches entire trust.

Gertrude Jekyll

Intuition is a suspension of logic due to impatience.

Rita Mae Brown

Patience and perseverance have a magical effect before which difficulties disappear and obstacles vanish.

John Quincy Adams

You can learn many things from children. How much patience you have, for instance.

Franklin P. Jones

I find hope in the darkest of days, and focus in the brightest. I do not judge the universe.

Tenzin Gyatso, 14th Dalai Lama

Patience is a question of putting others before oneself.

What wound did ever heal but by degrees?
William Shakespeare

Patience has its limits. Take it too far and it's cowardice.
George Jackson

We are what we repeatedly do. Excellence, then, is not an act but a habit.

Aristotle

Patience is sorrow's salve.

Charles Churchill

It takes patience to acquire good habits in life.

A healthy male adult bore consumes each year one and a half times his own weight in other people's patience.

John Updike

**Never a tear bedims the eye
That time and patience will not dry.**
Bret Harte

A man who is a master
of patience is master of
everything else.
George Savile

A statesman wants courage and a statesman wants vision; but believe me, after six months' experience, he wants first, second, third and all the time: patience.

Stanley Baldwin

Patience is the art of hoping against hope.

The keys to patience are acceptance and faith. Accept things as they are, and look realistically at the world around you. Have faith in yourself and in the direction you have chosen.

Ralph Marston

Affliction is the wholesome soil of virtue, where patience, honor, sweet humility, and calm fortitude, take root and strongly flourish.

David Mallet

Patience makes a woman beautiful in middle age.
Elliot Paul

Time heals all wounds.
Chaucer

As anyone who has ever been around a cat for any length of time well knows, cats have enormous patience with the limitations of the human kind.

Cleveland Amory

Deliberately seek opportunities for kindness, sympathy, and patience.

Evelyn Underhill

Simply by breathing, and by paying attention to our breath as it floods our bodies, filling us with life, we can find patience.

Even a happy life cannot be without a measure of darkness, and the word happy would lose its meaning if it were not balanced by sadness. Take things as they come along with patience and equanimity.

Carl Jung

Patience is passion tamed.

Lyman Abbott

Every great dream begins with a dreamer. Always remember, you have within you the strength, the patience, and the passion to reach for the stars to change the world.

Harriet Tubman

Everything in moderation,
including moderation.
Julia Child

**Patience is the support
of weakness; impatience
the ruin of strength.**

Charles Caleb Colton

Faith is not simply a patience that passively suffers until the storm is past. Rather, it is a spirit that bears things – with resignation, yes, but above all, with blazing, serene hope.

Corazon Aquino

There is a quiet beauty in the patient soul that the impatient among us fail to notice.

Patience is the art of concealing your impatience.

Guy Kawasaki

For anything worth having one must pay the price; and the price is always work, patience, love, self-sacrifice – no paper currency, no promises to pay, but the gold of real service.

John Burroughs

He that can have patience can have what he will.
Benjamin Franklin

Fortune knocks but once, but misfortune has much more patience.
Laurence J. Peter

Endurance is patience concentrated.

Thomas Carlyle

The secret of patience is finding something to do while you are waiting for something to happen.

He who rides the sea of the Nile must have sails woven of patience. *William Golding*

Heaven grant us patience with a man in love.

Rudyard Kipling

Patience, that blending of moral courage with physical timidity.

Thomas Hardy

Humility is attentive patience.

Simone Weil

Hopelessness has surprised me with patience.

Margaret J. Wheatley

**Patience is poultice
   to all wounds.
Sad Patience, too near
   neighbour to despair.**

Matthew Arnold

When travelling with someone, take a large dose of patience and tolerance with your morning coffee. *Helen Hayes*

The three 'P's: patience, passion, perseverance.

How many a man has thrown up his hands at a time when a little more effort, a little more patience would have achieved success?

Elbert Hubbard

I do not have much patience with a thing of beauty that must be explained to be understood. If it does need additional interpretation by someone other than the creator, then I question whether it has fulfilled its purpose.

Charlie Chaplin

Patience is a virtue
Possess it if you can
Seldom found in woman
Never in a man.

I've done an awful lot of stuff that's a monument to public patience.

Tyrone Power

Meekness: uncommon patience in planning a revenge that is worthwhile. *Ambrose Bierce*

I've worked so hard to eliminate the inner geek from my life. I suddenly realize I have no patience for those people who still have their geeks showing.

Kenny Loggins

Patience alone can conquer destiny.

If patience is worth anything, it must endure to the end of time. And a living faith will last in the midst of the blackest storm.

Mahatma Gandhi

Never run after a bus or a man.
There will always be another
one along in a minute.

If you have confidence you
have patience. Confidence,
that is everything. *Ilie Nastase*

All human wisdom is summed up in two words – wait and hope.

Alexandre Dumas

Knowing trees, I understand the meaning of patience. Knowing grass, I can appreciate persistence.

Hal Borland

The principle part of faith is patience.

George MacDonald

It seems likely that many of the young who don't wait for others to call them artists, but simply announce that they are, don't have the patience to make art.

Pauline Kael

It's a war of attrition. If you have patience and a modicum of faith in yourself your chances are not too bad.
Julie Bowen

You cannot walk with dignity if you are always in a hurry.

Endurance is nobler than strength, and patience than beauty.

John Ruskin

You're not allowed to be bossy when you're married. You have to learn compromise, and compassion and patience.

Star Jones

Only those who have patience to do simple things perfectly ever acquire the skill to do difficult things easily.

James J. Corbett

He who removes a mountain begins by carrying away small stones.

Chinese proverb

Our real blessings often appear to us in the shape of pains, losses and disappointments; but let us have patience and we soon shall see them in their proper figures.

Joseph Addison

Why should we live with such hurry and waste of life? We are determined to be starved before we are hungry.

Henry David Thoreau

One generation plants the trees. Another gets the shade.

Chinese proverb

Patience and tenacity are worth more than twice their weight of cleverness.

Thomas Huxley

When you do the common things in life in an uncommon way, you will command the attention of the world.

George Washington Carver

Patience is the ability to idle your motor when you feel like stripping your gears.

Barbara Johnson

There is no substitute for hard work, 23 or 24 hours a day. And there is no substitute for patience and acceptance.

César Chávez

Patience, persistence and perspiration make an unbeatable combination for success.

Napoleon Hill

Great oaks from little acorns grow.

The days of our lives, for all of us, are numbered. We know that. And yes, there are certainly times when we aren't able to muster as much strength and patience as we would like. It's called being human.

Elizabeth Edwards

Patience is the most overlooked and undervalued, but perhaps the most essential, of all the virtues.

The greatest power is often simple patience. *E. Joseph Cossman*

The first requirement of politics is not intellect or stamina but patience. Politics is a very long run game and the tortoise will usually beat the hare.
John Major

Keep on going, even when you can't see the end of the road.

The two most powerful warriors are patience and time. *Leo Tolstoy*

The key to everything is patience. You get the chicken by hatching the egg, not by smashing it.
Arnold H. Glasgow

The marvel of all history is the patience with which men and women submit to burdens unnecessarily laid upon them by their governments.

George Washington

There are three secrets to managing. The first secret is: have patience. The second is: be patient. And the third most important secret is: patience.

Chuck Tanner

If you can be patient in a moment of anger, you may escape months of sorrow.

There are very little things in this life I cannot afford and patience is one of them.

Larry Hagman

We have no patience with other people's vanity because it is offensive to our own.

François de La Rochefoucauld

With love and patience, nothing is impossible.

Daisaku Ikeda

Writing is good, thinking is better.
Cleverness is good, patience is better.
Hermann Hesse

You have to find the peace and patience within yourself to be a model and an example to others and not judge. *Judith Light*

Patience is the direct antithesis of anger.

Allan Lokos

The smallest brook runs into a river, which runs into the waters of the ocean.

Happy is he who learns to bear what he cannot change.

Johann Friedrich von Schiller

Showing patience to others, especially to children, is a form of loving respect.

All human errors are impatience, a premature breaking off of methodical procedure, an apparent fencing-in of what is apparently at issue.

Franz Kafka

It is to the one who endures that the final victory comes.

Buddha

In the end we are always rewarded for our good will, our patience, fair-mindedness, and gentleness with what is strange.

Friedrich Nietzsche

Patience is a virtue
Virtue is a grace
Both of them together
Make a pretty face.

Why is patience so important? Because it makes us pay attention.

Paulo Coelho

It is far better to endure patiently a smart which nobody feels but yourself, than to commit a hasty action whose evil consequences will extend to all connected with you. *Charlotte Brontë*

Kindness and patience go hand in hand.

Trees that are slow to grow bear the best fruit.

Molière

Tolerance is a form of immense patience, which it takes a lifetime to learn, and which is almost never perfected.

If I could store any character quality in a cookie jar, I'd store patience. Chocolate-chip patience cookies. And I'd eat them all at one sitting.
Jarod Kintz

Patience is not a virtue.
It's an achievement.
Vera Nazarian

If a man is destined to drown, he will drown even in a spoonful of water.

Jewish proverb

Those speak foolishly who ascribe their anger or their impatience to such as offend them or to tribulation. Tribulation does not make people impatient, but proves that they are impatient. So everyone may learn from tribulation how his heart is constituted.

Martin Luther

To rule one's anger is well; to prevent it is still better.

Tryon Edwards

An eternity is any moment opened with patience.

Noah Benshea

Learning
Self-Control

Until we have gained control over our own emotions – or 'passions', as earlier writers often called them – we cannot control the direction of our lives. This section explores the many connections between patience and mastery over oneself, whether in our day-to-day experiences, or in our spiritual lives.

Start with the simple tasks; progress slowly to the more difficult. With patience, they will seem easy by the time you get there.

Don't think that, just because others achieve more than you do, they're necessarily more gifted. Sometimes, they simply have more confidence, more patience and more capacity for hard work.

Patience is not a quality you have; it's a quality you make.

Self-respect is the root of discipline: the sense of dignity grows with the ability to say no to oneself.

Abraham Heschel

To build patience is to build mastery.

It takes patience to recognize that you are sometimes at fault; patience with yourself, and the humility to resolve that you will do better in the future.

We can only create what we can anticipate.

Discipline weighs ounces, regret weighs tons.

Infinite patience brings immediate results.

Wayne Dyer

Whatever your troubles, have the patience to notice the beauty of the world around you. Take a walk outside, perhaps in a park or in the countryside, and let nature refresh your spirits.

Not being able to govern events, I govern myself, and apply myself to them, if they will not apply themselves to me.

Michel de Montaigne

Nobody's perfect.
So have patience!

Self-control isn't the same as bottling up your feelings. It's about learning to recognize your anger; and the situations that trigger it, and being able to decide for yourself whether, and how, you wish to express it – instead of flying off the handle right away.

A patient person can always see the future in the present.

It is a man's own mind, not his enemy or foe, that lures him to evil ways.

Buddha

You can't have your cake and eat it. Patience is recognizing that you have made your choices in life, of your own free will, and that means you may have had to turn down other opportunities.

How many times a day do we have to tell ourselves, 'Wait. Not yet'. It's called patience, learning to discipline yourself so that you get what you really want – long-term satisfaction, a sense of fulfilment, rather than simply giving in to your desire for instant gratification, right now.

It's all right letting yourself go, as long as you can get yourself back.
Mick Jagger

Whatever your goal, there will always be setbacks and disappointments along the way. The patient man or woman recognizes this, and continues to move forward come what may, slowly but surely.

Patience is the road to freedom, and self-mastery is its reward.

Patience: an open mind; a willingness to learn; the enthusiasm to attempt new tasks; courage in the face of failure; the humility to accept one's mistakes; and the resilience to carry on.

I am indeed
a king because
I know how to
rule myself.

Pietro Aretino

Waiting is often
harder than
working.

When you feel impatient, ask yourself, is this sense of urgency going to help me get my task done quicker – or will it just slow me down?

If someone makes you angry, begin by telling yourself to keep your voice calm and level. It's suprising how much difference this can make. Human beings, like animals, respond first and foremost to tone of voice, rather than exactly what you say.

Serving one's own passions is the greatest slavery.

Thomas Fuller

When you lose your temper, you lose touch with the part of yourself that is rational and kind. In this way, you lose part of yourself.

Impatience implies a lack of confidence: in oneself, and in other people. It is a way of showing that you do not really believe there is a solution to the problem, and that you have given up finding ways of working towards it.

The only time losing is more fun than winning is when you're fighting temptation.

Tom Wilson

The hardest lesson we have to learn in life is how to get on with ourselves.

Those who are easily offended are often insensitive to the offence that they cause others.

If passion drives you, let reason hold the reins.
Benjamin Franklin

Learn from adversity; let it be a lesson in patience rather than despair.

The time will come when winter will ask you what you were doing all summer. *Henry Clay*

Patience is having the confidence to quietly let someone know when he or she is irritating you in a small way – before the irritation builds to anger and impatience.

The sooner I fall behind, the more time I have to catch up.

The difference between try and triumph is a little umph.

The artist is nothing without the gift, but the gift is nothing without the work.

Emile Zola

Opportunity may only knock once, but temptation leans on the doorbell.

Sometimes we try too hard to be patient, only to let our anger build up to the point where we explode. Learn to avoid this situation, by having the courage to express your feelings, in a calm, polite way, before you get angry.

Efficiency is intelligent laziness.
David Dunham

In order to learn patience, children need first to be shown it.

A promise is a cloud. Fulfilment is rain.

Arabian proverb

Do it, and then you will feel motivated to do it. *Zig Ziglar*

You cannot plough a field by turning it over in your mind.

There is a difference between seeing and noticing; between hearing and listening; between touching and feeling. That difference is patience.

Success is a ladder you cannot climb with your hands in your pockets.

It is an undoubted truth that, the less one has to do, the less time one finds to do it in.

Earl of Chesterfield

There is much that we do not understand, about ourselves and other people. Accept that sometimes, we will rub each other up the wrong way, without meaning to, and that, with goodwill, we can forgive and forget.

Routines can be boring and hard to follow. Find small ways to vary them, or to improve their efficiency. That way, you will help yourself to be disciplined about them.

A good example is more effective than good advice.

You may delay, but time will not.
Benjamin Franklin

Nobody likes the initial sensation of diving into a cold swimming pool, or going out for a run in the rain. But once you're in your stride, you'll start to enjoy it – and you'll feel great once you're in the shower afterwards!

Improvements begin with 'I'.

Arnold Glasgow

If you have no will to change something, you have no right to criticize it.

If you have much, give of your wealth.
If you have little, give of your heart.
Arabian proverb

Between saying and doing many a pair of shoes is worn out.

Italian proverb

Much good work is lost for the lack of a little more.

Edward H. Harriman

Talk doesn't cook rice.

Chinese proverb

Being good is commendable, but only when it is combined with doing good is it useful.

Patience is a great confidence builder. It reminds us that we do not always need to be super-talented or skilled; often, hard work and 'stickability' is enough.

Nobody can do everything, but everybody can do something.

The Wisdom of the Ancients

In the classical era, patience was regarded as one of the major virtues, and much was written about its importance, not just for great leaders and thinkers, but for the ordinary man and woman, too. In this collection, you'll find some of the most pithy sayings from ancient Eastern and Western culture, many of which are still in use today, since they still continue to be relevant to life in the 21st century.

Have patience with all things, but chiefly have patience with yourself. Do not lose courage in considering your own imperfections but instantly set about remedying them – every day, begin the task anew.

St Francis de Sales

Patience is the greatest of all virtues.

Cato the Elder

A wise man is superior to any insults which can be put upon him, and the best reply to unseemly behaviour is patience and moderation.

Molière

The fates have given mankind a patient soul.

Homer

If I have ever made any valuable discoveries, it has been owing more to patient attention than to any other talent. *Isaac Newton*

Patience is the companion of wisdom.

St Augustine

Upon the heat and flame of thy distemper sprinkle cool patience.

William Shakespeare

Patience can conquer destiny.

Hope is patience with the lamp lit.

Tertullian

I have just three things to teach: simplicity, patience, compassion. These three are your greatest treasures.

Lao Tzu

Patience is the best remedy for every trouble.

Plautus

All things come to him who waits.

It is easier to find men who will volunteer to die, than to find those who are willing to endure pain with patience.

Julius Caesar

Patience and time do more than strength or passion.

Jean de la Fontaine

To bear with patience wrongs done to oneself is a mark of perfection, but to bear with patience wrongs done to someone else is a mark of imperfection and even of actual sin.

Thomas Aquinas

Who ever is out of patience is out of possession of their soul.

Francis Bacon

If we are facing in the right direction, all we have to do is keep on walking.

Buddhist saying

A loving heart abides in a patient soul.

A handful of patience is worth more than a bushel of brains.

Dutch proverb

Experience has taught me this, that we undo ourselves by impatience. Misfortunes have their life and their limits, their sickness and their health.

Michel de Montaigne

Festina lente –
more haste, less speed.

The drops of rain make a hole in the stone not by violence but by oft falling.

Lucretius

Our patience will achieve more than our force.
Edmund Burke

Where there is no enemy within, the enemies outside cannot hurt you.

African proverb

Whatever we learn to do, we learn by actually doing it; men come to be builders, for instance, by building, and harp players by playing the harp. In the same way, by doing just acts we come to be just; by doing self-controlled acts, we come to be self-controlled; and by doing brave acts, we become brave.

Aristotle

To be impatient is to be a coward in the face of fortune

Beware the fury of a patient man.

John Dryden

I have come into this world to see this:
the sword drops from men's hands
even at the height of their arc of rage
because we have finally realized
there is just one flesh we can wound.

Hafiz

No road is too long for him who advances slowly and does not hurry, and no attainment is beyond his reach who equips himself with patience to achieve it.

Jean de La Bruyère

Anger is a short madness.

Horace

Holding on to anger is like grasping a hot coal with the intent of throwing it at someone else; you are the one who gets burned.
Buddha

People of little understanding are most apt to be angry when their sense is called into question.

Samuel Richardson

If you have a wounded heart, touch it as little as you would an injured eye. There are only two remedies for the suffering of the soul: hope and patience.

Pythagoras

The intoxication of anger, like that of the grape, shows us to others, but hides us from ourselves.

John Dryden

Nothing in excess.

Chilon

How much more grievous are the consequences of anger than the causes of it.

Marcus Aurelius

Learning without reflection is a waste, reflection without learning is dangerous.

Confucius

Never move quickly – except to avoid work or find excuses!

Young men err in everything by excess and vehemence, contrary to the precept of Chilon; they do all things too much, since they love and hate too much, and likewise in everything else. They fancy and insist that they know all things, and this is why they overdo everything.

Aristotle

Poor is the man who cannot find time for patience.

Patience serves as a protection against wrongs as clothes do against cold. For if you put on more clothes as the cold increases, it will have no power to hurt you. So in like manner you must grow in patience when you meet with great wrongs, and they will then be powerless to vex your mind.

Leonardo da Vinci

Everywhere man blames nature and fate, yet his fate is mostly but the echo of his character and passions, his mistakes and weaknesses.

Democritus

For everything there is a season,
And a time for every purpose under heaven:
A time to be born, and a time to die;
A time to plant, and a time to pluck up what is
    planted;
A time to weep, and a time to laugh;
A time to mourn, and a time to dance;
A time to seek, and a time to lose;
A time to keep silence, and a time to speak;
A time to love, and a time to hate,
A time for war, and a time for peace.

The Bible

One is rich not through one's possessions, but through that which one can with dignity do without.

Epicurus

Genius is eternal patience.

Michaelangelo

Mix a little foolishness with your prudence: it's good to be silly at the right moment.

Horace

All things are difficult before they are easy.

He who submits to fate without complaint is wise.

Euripides

Patience is bitter, but its fruit is sweet.

Jean-Jacques Rousseau

It is not good for all your wishes to be fulfilled: through sickness you recognize the value of health, through evil the value of good, through hunger satisfaction, through exertion, the value of rest.

Heraclitus

Bear patiently, my heart – for you have suffered heavier things.

Homer

If man is moderated and contented, then even age is no burden; if he is not, then even youth is full of cares.

Plato

A pleasant and happy life does not come from external things: man draws from within himself, as from a spring, pleasure and joy.

Plutarch

You must learn to walk before you can run.

There is only one step from the sublime to the ridiculous.

Napoleon

Remember, no human condition is ever permanent: then you will not be overjoyed in good fortune, nor too sorrowful in misfortune.
Socrates

A watched pot never boils.

Lovely it is, when the winds are churning up the waves on the great sea, to gaze out from the land on the great efforts of someone else.

Lucretius

To have begun is half the job: be bold and be sensible.

Horace

Fall seven times, stand up eight.

Japanese proverb

Rome wasn't built in a day.

A man's character is his fate.

Heraclitus

Give me but one firm spot on which to stand, and I will move the earth.

Archimedes

Taking Your Time

The modern world is speeding up, but we are constantly told, for the sake of our mental and physical health, to slow down. How do we achieve that, without ducking our work and family responsibilities? Well, here we show you how to adopt a new attitude, so that life stops being a race against the clock, and begins, instead, to be a matter of slow but sure progress.

Everybody wants to be somebody. Have the patience to be yourself.

Slow down. Ask yourself, in ten years' time, will it matter whether I was a little behind in my schedule today?

Listen to your breath. Breathe in, slowly, through your nose; and out again. Feel your breath filling your lungs, filling your body with energy.

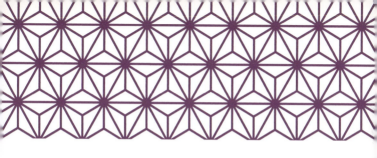

Be not afraid of growing slowly;
only of standing still.
Chinese proverb

**If you lack patience, you will also
lack foresight, the ability to see
the consequences of a certain
action, or situation, in advance.**

To be in a hurry is to kill your talent. If you wish to reach the sun, it isn't enough to jump impulsively into the air.

Peter Ustinov

A teacher may sometimes get her pupils' attention by lowering her voice, rather than by shouting. That's because they are curious about what she is saying, and have to listen to find out.

A bad workman blames his tools.

Good health is a matter of luck, of course, but also of patience. Only by adhering to a healthy routine will you give yourself a better chance of living to a ripe old age.

Impatience is a dead end; patience a destination.

Learning to think about your responsibilities before you fulfil your desires is a matter of patience, experience, and self-discipline.

When one door closes, another opens; but we so often look so long and so regretfully upon the closed door, that we do not see the ones which open for us.

Alexander Graham Bell

Better to remain silent
and be thought a fool,
than to open your mouth
and remove all doubt.

What good is
impatience?
About as useful as
banging your head
against a brick wall.

The dawn does not break suddenly, but by degrees. Waiting for the sun to come up in the morning, watching the light on the horizon grow brighter, is an act of patience that may bring great joy.

Patience is a gift; pass it on.

There is nothing more galling to angry people than the coolness of those on whom they wish to vent their spleen.

Alexandre Dumas

Those without patience may love deeply, but the people they love will not necessarily benefit from that love.

To tame a wild animal, even a robin in your garden, you will need patience, gentleness, and care.

Give a man a fish and you feed him for a day; teach a man to fish, and you feed him for a lifetime.

The man for whom time stretches out painfully is one waiting in vain, disappointed at not finding tomorrow already continuing yesterday.

Theodor Adorno

Those with patience know that they will not have to wait forever; those without it, feel as if they already have been waiting too long.

Learning self-discipline and self-control is simply a way of being patient with yourself.

Observe the postage stamp. Its usefulness depends on its ability to stick to one thing until it gets there.

Henry Wheeler Shaw

The card game Patience is a game that you play by yourself. It is so named because it requires patience; but it teaches patience, too.

Be tolerant of others. Not everyone is the same. If people behave in a way you don't like or understand, give them the benefit of the doubt. Remind yourself that you know far less about the circumstances of their lives than they do.

Only by testing our patience do we discover the limits of it.

If you are patient with people, you will find it easier to work with them.

There are no honours too distant to the man who prepares himself for them with patience.

Jean de la Bruyère

Having patience is a way of slowing time down. And, if you can do that without getting restless and bored, you will have found a way of making the days of your life more enjoyable.

Instead of finding fault, try to find patience.

There's no need to pull up a flower to check whether its roots are healthy; you can see that they are by the way it blooms.

Time is a created thing.
To say, ' I don't have time', is like saying, 'I don't want to'.
Lao Tzu

Think the best of others before you think the worst.

Humility is attentive patience.

Simone Weil

Thinking that you know what someone is like before you have taken the trouble to find out is a sign of impatience. Taking an interest shows patience, and a measure of respect for individuality.

Measure twice, cut once.

Patience is the ability to put up with people you'd like to put down.

The patient person sits quietly and observes; the impatient person is too concerned with self to notice what is going on.

Patience is a firm refusal to give up or give in, even in the face of tremendous odds.

Nature gave us one tongue and two ears so we could hear twice as much as we speak.

Epictetus

The outcome of patience is trust and tolerance.

In order to learn any skill, however easy, at least a modicum of patience is needed.

Sit quietly. Focus your mind on an object. Let your thoughts come and go, without judging them. It's difficult, but with patience, you will learn … to be patient.

I value the friend who finds time for me on his calendar. But I cherish the friend who does not consult his calendar.

Robert Brault

There are no endings: only new beginnings.

Patience is the freedom to live at your own pace and in your own way, without obeying the demands of the crammed schedule set for you or that you have foolishly set for yourself.

Patience is about not judging yourself or others too harshly. It is about love, rather than anger; about tranquillity, rather than activity.

God's gifts put man's best dreams to shame.

Elizabeth Barrett Browning

With patience, we can begin to transcend the daily irritations and annoyances that threaten to make our lives stressful and tense, and that threaten to harm our relationships with others.

Vision without action is a daydream. Action without vision is a nightmare.

Japanese proverb

The time to be happy is now; the place to be happy is here.

Robert G. Ingersoll

Well begun is half done.

Patience is greatly valued by the major world religions, for it is essential in spiritual life, as well as in dealing with practical issues.

Opportunity is waiting, you need but to open the door.

Encountering a frustrating person, or situation, can offer a chance for you to look inward at yourself and begin to recognize patterns in your own behaviour: for example, being over-critical; being easily offended; feeling powerless to change matters; and so on.

Enjoy your own life without comparing it to that of another.
Marquis de Condorcet

Winning is earning. Losing is learning.

Be mindful of thoughts, because
  thoughts will become words.
Be mindful of words, because words
  will become plans.
Be mindful of plans, because plans
  will become actions.
Be mindful of actions, because
  actions will become habits.
Be mindful of habits, because habits
  will become character.

Let life unfold. Try not to rush. The
future is a mirage that will disappear
as you come close to it.

**Two roads diverged in a wood, and –
I took the one less travelled by
And that has made all the difference.**

Robert Frost

Patience is not about being passive. It is a conscious decision to recognize the weaknesses and difficulties others may have, and to make allowances for them, as often as possible.

Write injuries in the sand, kindness in marble.

We always hope to get a lot done in the day, so that there will be a chance to relax and enjoy life. But what if the list is too long? Instead of waiting until we have finished our tasks, perhaps we should consider enjoying the ride.

**Perseverance is not one long race;
it is many short races, one after another!**

Walter Elliott

In the first minute that follows an irritating remark, ask yourself, is the irritating person actually responding to you, or simply being insensitive?

The longest mile is the last mile home.

Life is what happens to you while you're busy making other plans.

John Lennon

True knowledge comes to those who are patient; the impatient find only false dogmas and shallow philosophies.

A still tongue makes a wise head.

However hard you find it to be patient, don't give up. Every day is a new beginning.

The teacher has not taught until the student has learned.

We don't exist in a vacuum. Our time is constantly taken up with the needs of others. Sometimes it takes a lot of patience not to resent that intrusion.

Our greatest glory is not that we never fall, but that we rise every time we fall.

Confucius

Rather be a dog in peace than a man in war.

Chinese proverb

Knee-jerk reactions, such as losing your temper, are usually harmful.
Try to act with intention, rather than get caught off guard by your anger.

When a child is whining, step back and ask yourself, what is it that he or she really wants here? Can you remember back to a time when you were like that? How did it feel not to be heard?

At the core of every true talent there is an awareness of the difficulties inherent in any achievement, and the confidence that by persistence and patience something worthwhile will be realized. *Eric Hoffer*

Prior preparation prevents poor performance.

None of us are perfect.
If you're in a bad mood,
sometimes it's a good idea just
to acknowledge that – and
apologize for being grumpy.

Revenge is a dish best served cold.

Patience shows we accept the fact that events unfold at their own pace. And that we are here to witness that process, wherever it may lead.

We all need goals, but try not to live in the future. With patience, you can find a way to work towards your ambitions without sacrificing your appreciation of the present moment.

Good ideas are not adopted automatically. They must be driven into practice with courageous patience.

Hyman Rickover

Each day, expect just a little more
from yourself than you did yesterday.

The impatient person is concerned with how quickly we move towards our goal; the patient one with how effectively we do so.

Thinking big means starting small.

There is a correlation between impatience and greed, in that both assume there is never enough – whether in terms of time, or of what you desire.

Patience cannot heal sorrow, but it can make it lighter to bear.

To step back, look at where you are in life, understand how you have progressed to this point, and think about the changes you need to make, takes patience and understanding.

Far better to bite your lip than to bite someone's head off.

When we hurt other people, it is usually because we have failed to show them the patience, respect, and sensitivity that every individual deserves.

A patient horse will carry the rider far.

If you don't have the patience to listen to both sides of an argument, you will be unable to reach a decision guided by truth.

To have run out of patience is to have run out of hope.

What kind of person did you want to be when you were a child? Are you that person now? Sometimes, realizing that we are a person the child in us would have liked and admired can make us feel more patient with the difficulties we face every day.

If you would know strength and patience, welcome the company of trees.
Hal Borland

Today could be the day that you have waited so patiently for.

Accepting the fact that sometimes things go wrong, and that there is no one particularly to blame, is an important step on the road to becoming patient.

We shall escape
the uphill by never
turning back.
Christina Rossetti

Patience is
faith in the
future.

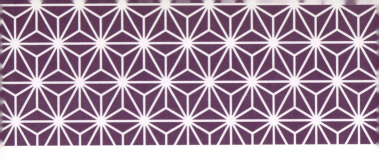

Every man must patiently bide his time. He must wait – not in listless idleness but in constant, steady, cheerful endeavours, always willing and fulfilling and accomplishing his task, that when the occasion comes he may be equal to the occasion.

Henry Wadsworth Longfellow

A lazy horse will break his back rather than make two journeys.

Failure is not always disastrous; sometimes, it can signify that there may be a better way for you to move forward than the one that you chose.

To get quick results, take time and care. Use patience.

Beware of endeavouring to become a great man in a hurry. One such attempt in ten thousand may succeed. These are fearful odds.

Benjamin Disraeli

It is not so much what you say that matters, as how you say it. Using a quiet, respectful tone of voice will often allow you to express yourself honestly without causing offence.

The ability to make thoughtful, sensible decisions while under pressure is called patience.

Patience is yours to give, not for others to take.

A young person, to achieve, must first get out of his mind any notion either of the ease or rapidity of success. Nothing ever just happens in this world.

Edward William Bok

Patience is the hardest lesson for a headstrong child to learn.

Having patience gives us the freedom to consider our immediate circumstances, rather than simply to concentrate on our ambitions for the future.

Make do and mend.

Having patience is not the same as being dispassionate or removed. Having patience means caring very much, but not allowing one's desires to dominate.

Keep your anger to yourself, but share your serenity with others. *Dalai Lama*

Patience is the key to the door of contentment.

Patience is not the absence of conflict, but the quality that allows us to deal with conflict in a creative and peaceful way.

If you can't change your fate, change your attitude.
Amy Tan

Some pleasures are worth waiting a long time for; like grapes on the vine, they grow sweeter as they mature.

Sometimes patience is the only choice you can make, until other choices become possible.

Truth is power, but only when one has patience and requires of it no immediate effect.

Romano Guardini

Patience moves mountains; anger creates them.

The test of good manners is to be patient with bad ones.

Solomon Ibn Gabirol

Learning patience is a lifelong quest for a goal that is seldom, if ever, reached.

How do you feel when you are angry? Bitter, unsatisfied, at odds with life. And when you are patient? At peace with the world, and with your fellow human beings.

Let it be.

We should remember that every opportunity to develop anger is also an opportunity to develop patience.

Geshe Kelsang Gyatso

Patience is a river flowing from a spring that never runs dry.

You will learn more from listening to others talk about themselves than by talking about yourself.

Impatience frequently leads to misunderstanding, and discord; patience to tolerance, and harmony.

Self-reverence, self-knowledge, self-control – these three alone lead life to sovereign power.

Alfred Lord Tennyson

Little By Little

Patience is an ingredient in most great endeavours, simply because taking one step at a time, little by little, is often the most effective way to get the job done. But it's sometimes hard to see the small improvements we make day to day; unless, of course, we make a mental note to do so – and then put our knowledge into practice.

The high achievers of the world are not necessarily the most talented. They're just the ones who carry on, long after everyone else has quit and gone home.

It is patience that lends us the strength to endure.

The world, and other people, are not under your control. At most, you only have influence over a tiny corner of existence. Once you have understood that, you can relax and be patient.

However long the night, the dawn will break.

African proverb

Even the knowledge of my own fallibility cannot keep me from making mistakes. Only when I fall do I get up again.

Vincent van Gogh

A patient enemy is the most dangerous kind.

Encouragement, the ability to be positive even when the going is slow, is a form of patience that shows love and compassion.

Looking at small advantages prevents great affairs from being accomplished.
Confucius

Learning patience is an act of love.

Since we cannot get what we like, let us like what we can get.

A thankful heart is not only the greatest virtue, but the parent of all the other virtues. *Cicero*

The greatest gifts that you can give a child are your love, your time, and your patience.

Take pleasure in the little things of life.

Patience tells us that there is a time and a place for telling home truths, and that in order to help, not to hurt, we have to wait for that time.

What a fool does at the end, the wise do in the beginning.

Each human being on the planet is a work in progress. With patience, that work can be continued, but it will never be finished.

In reality, humility means nothing other than complete honesty about yourself.

William Countryman

There are times when it's best to keep your opinions to yourself. That takes patience, and sensitivity towards the feelings of other people.

Do not seek for eternal happiness. Instead, be aware of the moments of happiness that come to you.

Understanding requires patience, especially where your fellow human beings are concerned.

When we get impatient and angry at the faults of others, we do well to remember that it is often the same faults in ourselves that we really find infuriating, and that annoy us so much.

Tomorrow is often the busiest day of the week.

Spanish proverb

He is rich who owns the day, and no one owns the day who allows it to be invaded with fret and anxiety.

Ralph Waldo Emerson

Just because you're right, doesn't mean to say that everyone else is wrong. Have the patience to allow others their own opinions, and don't try to stifle them with yours.

People live differently. In most cases, there is no wrong or right about it. Recognize that if people differ from you in their values, customs, and habits, they are not doing so to undermine your way of life.

Keep your feet on the ground and your thoughts at lofty heights.

Peace Pilgrim

Each human being in the world is unique and should be valued as such. It takes patience to really believe that, especially when people behave badly, and to put one's belief into action.

It's easy to be negative, to think the worst. To be positive sometimes takes an effort of will, an ability to see the opportunities life presents, even at the most difficult times, and a great deal of patience and perseverance.

Diligence is the mother of good luck.
Benjamin Franklin

More grows in the garden than the gardener knows he has sown.

Little by little, through patience and repeated effort, the mind will become stilled in the self.
Bhagavad Gita

What is love, except the patience to overlook our loved ones' faults, and to go on loving them just the same?

Anger is the enemy of non-violence and pride is a monster that swallows it up.
Mahatma Gandhi

The business of forging harmonious links between people, whether it takes place at the level of nations, of communities, or individuals, depends not only on goodwill but on patience.

If you can't say anything nice, say nothing at all.

Trust yourself. You know more than you think you do.

Benjamin Spock

Some people find it easy to think of others; some are more bound up with themselves. If you belong to the second category, don't beat yourself up – you may have other qualities, such as being singleminded in achieving your goals. Have patience with yourself, and recognize that you will need to make a special effort to be sensitive to the needs of those around you.

The most successful people are those who are good at Plan B.

James Yorke

Being a fair judge in a dispute, whether between children, between family members, friends, or at work, means listening patiently to both sides of the argument before you give your opinion.

It is better to prevent than cure.

Making friends is all about getting to know people. And to get to know someone well, you need to listen patiently, so that you can find out who that person is.

If you look for faults in others, you will always find them.

When you come to the end of your rope, tie a knot, and hang on.

Franklin D. Roosevelt

Ignorance often comes down to impatience and intolerance; the inability to slow down, open our hearts and minds, and learn about the world around us.

Little by little, one walks far.

Peruvian proverb

Bear with people that irritate you; do your best not to be unkind.

The abiding virtue of humility is that it reminds you of your fallibility, and your deep connection with the rest of humanity.

Learning patience can be difficult, especially for people who are naturally impetuous. But the result may be that you can achieve your goals, and become a kinder, more tolerant person in the process.

Success is not final, failure is not fatal; it is the courage to continue that counts.

Winston Churchill

Nothing teaches us patience like the experience of having, or caring for, young children. They test our patience daily, hourly, minute by minute; yet they are completely dependent on our kindness and forbearance.

Arriving at one point is the starting point to another.
John Dewey

Patience and humility come as a set –
you can't have one without the other.

Little changes
lead, over
time, to great
changes.

Patience is not an abstract concept. We learn it by practising it, every day.

If your actions inspire others to dream more, learn more, do more, and become more, you are a leader.

John Quincy Adams

You can always make time for the things that matter.

The beauties of the natural world do not always unfold before your eyes. Sometimes, it takes patience to see them: to watch and wait for a bird to come into your garden; to notice the slow growth of a plant or flower; to plan for the season ahead, or the one after that.

A child learns to walk first by crawling, then by standing up, and falling over. The process takes a long time, and a lot of effort.

Tell yourself, every day I grow and learn a little bit more.

Any fool can criticize, condemn, and blame but it takes character and self-control to be understanding and forgiving. *Dale Carnegie*

The more patience you have, the more joy you will experience when you finally achieve what you have worked so hard for.

Slowing
Down

'More haste, less speed', as the old saying goes, and it's still true today. Taking life at a slower pace doesn't necessarily mean that we get less done; in fact, we may find that it is a great deal more productive in the long run. In this section, we ask, what's all the rush? Why let life go by so fast when you can slow down and enjoy the ride?

The slower you run, the longer you can go on running, and the farther you will go.

Patience is realizing that you can't control the whole world. Sometimes, you just have to sit it out, and hope for the best.

When you allow your impatience to get the better of you, you show you have little self-respect.

It is important, from time to time, to slow down, to go away by yourself, and simply be.

Eileen Caddy

Patience: in good times, the capacity to be tolerant and good-tempered; in bad times, the emotional resources to endure pain and suffering calmly, and with dignity.

When you've got a difficult problem to solve, don't panic: slow down, and give yourself time to think about it.

Little by little achieves a lot.

Breathe. Let go. And remind yourself that this very moment is the only one you know you have for sure. *Oprah Winfrey*

Being patient is not a sign of giving up, or giving in. It simply means that one bears difficult situations with dignity and grace.

Patience is not a sign of weakness, but of strength.

There must be quite a few things that a hot bath won't cure, but I don't know many of them.

Sylvia Plath

Patience is like a flower: tend it carefully, and it will grow.

Cultivate a habit of patience; so that, when it becomes a habit, you won't even need to think about it.

Don't be discouraged by day-to-day problems; be confident in your belief that, if you carry on working towards your goal, you will eventually achieve it.

The art of living lies less in eliminating our troubles than in growing with them.

Bernard M. Baruch

Keep on keeping on.

Ask yourself, do you want what you don't have; or what you can't have?

If people concentrated on the really important things of life, there'd be a shortage of fishing poles.

Doug Larson

The Creator didn't do it all in one day. What makes me think I can?

Nothing is worth more than this day.

Johann Wolfgang von Goethe

Patience is about taking a reality check from time to time: thinking about what is viable and practical before you decide to act.

A life spent in constant labour is a life wasted, save a man be such a fool as to regard a fulsome obituary notice as ample reward.

George Jean Nathan

In creative work, the job is never finished. It is never enough, and it is never as good as it could be. Understanding that, and learning to live with it, is an act of patience.

Who will tell whether one happy moment of love or the joy of breathing or walking on a bright morning and smelling the fresh air, is not worth all the suffering and effort which life implies?

Erich Fromm

Tension is who you think you should be.
Relaxation is who you are.

Stress should be a powerful driving force, not an obstacle.

Bill Phillips

Things turn out best when you make the best of the way things turn out.

You don't always need to tell people when they are being foolish; in most cases, they will find out soon enough, all by themselves.

Slow down in life. Live; breathe; and learn.

Difficulties are meant to rouse, not discourage. The human spirit is to grow strong by conflict.

William Ellery Channing

The most satisfying rest is the one we have earned after a hard day's work.

Most people achieved their greatest success one step beyond what looked like their greatest failure.

For fast-acting relief, try slowing down.

Lily Tomlin

Knowing when to accept, and when to refuse, is a mystery that only the patient understand.

Smile; forgive; forget; but most of all, keep moving on.

Successful people fail many more times than unsuccessful ones.

Time is but the stream I go a-fishing in.

Henry David Thoreau

If things aren't going right today, there is always tomorrow. Have patience, and your time will come.

You will not be punished for your anger; you will be punished by your anger.

Buddha

Harsh words that are spoken may be quickly forgotten; harsh words that are written down remain etched on the mind for ever.

Never write a letter in anger; or, if you do, don't post it.

Stress is an ignorant state; it believes everything is an emergency.

Natalie Goldberg

Put off your anger until tomorrow; that's the only kind of procrastination that is helpful in life.

No one can hammer a nail into a wall with just one blow.

The art of love is largely the art of persistence.

Albert Ellis

Patience: the ability to deal with impatience.

If you're stressed and overworked, force yourself to take a break. You'll come back with your batteries recharged, more able to cope.

The difference between perseverance and obstinacy is that one often comes from a strong will, and the other from a strong won't.

Henry Ward Beecher

Walk more slowly. Talk more slowly. You will see more, and make more sense.

Patience is a kind of dignity: the ability to endure and to forbear, without constant complaint.

To learn patience, you must first learn humility.

Illness may be nature's way of telling you to slow down.

Time goes, you say, Ah no! Alas time stays, we go. *Henry Austin Dobson*

We all know when it's time to slow down and take it easy. But some of us can't stop.

Whether or not you enjoy sport, if you take the trouble to notice the small improvements your body makes when you take regular exercise, week by week, in terms of strength, flexibility, and power, you will begin to take pleasure in it.

Rest is not idleness, and to lie sometimes on the grass under trees on a summer's day, listening to the murmur of the water, or watching the clouds float across the sky, is by no means a waste of time.

John Lubbock

No pain, no gain.

There are times when we all need a 'news blackout'. Switch off your TV, computer, or phone, and just forget, for a day, what's going on in the world.

All know the way; few actually walk it.

Bodhidharma